ACCESS TO CASH | WEALTH | POWER

ACCESS TO CASH

Don't fight forces, use them.

— Buckminster Fuller

Money is usually attracted, not pursued.

— Jim Rohn

The reason I've been able to be so financially successful is my focus has never, even for one minute been money.

— Oprah Winfrey

You can't use up creativity.
The more you use the more you have.

— Maya Angelou

Instead of thinking outside of the box,
get rid of the box.

— Deepak Chopra

Money is a certificate of performance received for serving people and making their lives better.

— Rabbi Daniel Lapin

PRAISE

for the *Money & You* book series

"Thank you so much, Doria Cordova! What a gift you are! The principle of leverage that you teach in this book has helped me generate over US$10 million dollars liquid, exponentially grow my team, and find the peace I was searching for."

— Dame Nicola Smith-Jackson, CEO and Founder
Pink Millionaire Club

"Money & You made a huge impact in my life. I learned to correct what doesn't work – to cooperate – time management – about agreements – about integrity. It was a huge quantum-leap experience for me. If you look at anyone who is big in the human potential movement, they all took Money & You."

— Jack Canfield, *Chicken Soup for the Soul* Book Series

"Money & You's work in education is powerful, profound, and life-changing. I salute their efforts, and I recommend it highly."

— Anthony Robbins, *Awaken the Giant Within*

"Once you understand the power (and paramount availability) of ACCESS, your life will change for the better! I highly recommend Doria's timeless work…"

— Dr. John Gray, *Mars / Venus Book Series*

"Money & You changed my life and redirected my business career. The program is more about discovering ourselves than it is about money, yet in the process I learned more about money than I ever dreamed possible."

— Robert Kiyosaki, Co-author, *Rich Dad Poor Dad* Series

PRAISE

for the *Money & You* book series

"You are either in control of your money…or your money is in control of you. Access to Cash gives you the framework to take control of your money. Dame Doria continues to provide life-changing education. From the Money & You programs to the Access to Cash book, she has dedicated her life to helping others create financial freedom."

— Sharon Lechter, CEO *Pay Your Family First*, Co-author *Rich Dad Poor Dad* Series

"Money & You is one of the most brilliant trainings in the world. I took it, learned, and earned vastly more because of it."

— Mark Victor Hansen, *Chicken Soup for the Soul* Series

"Thank you, Doria, for teaching me how to express that which I truly desired. It worked beyond my expectations. I now have successful multi-million-dollar businesses, I have a beautiful life partner and two gorgeous children.
And I now lead Excellerated programs!"

— Andrew Barron, Managing Director *PTP Group*

"Access to Cash is a must-read for entrepreneurs! Dame Doria Cordova offers grounded support around money and leverage strategies to help you grow your money. Additionally, she delves into mindset strategies to help you create wealth in your life."

— Dame Maria Simone, Founder *ZenMoose Capital*

PRAISE

for the *Money & You* book series

"Through the principles and guidance received from this book and Money & You, I've been able to take my business from zero to fifty people in the last three years, from $0 in revenue to multiple millions in three years."

— Dr. Jay Pandya, Founder and CEO *Masterdojo*

"Too many entrepreneurs fail to make the important impact that is their true purpose because they lack the important skill of accessing cash. Grab this book and read it quickly. Then put it into practice to access cash and grow fast!'

— JV Crum III, Founder, *ConsciousMillionaire.com* – Host, *Conscious Millionaire Show*

"Access to Cash makes financial literacy easy. A condensed book that doesn't have fillers but only focuses on what the reader needs to know to move forward with a more abundant and prosperous financial life."

— Moe Rock, CEO and Publisher
The Los Angeles Tribune

"Access to Cash is absolutely a must-read for any entrepreneur who wants to quantum leap their ability to leverage money and become magnetic to exponential financial resources. Dame Doria's new book is a perfect complement to her life-changing program, Money & You."

— Jennifer Hough, President of *The Wide Awakening*

PRAISE

for the *Money & You* book series

"Doria, her books, and her teachings have allowed me to collapse time frames on learning curves and achieve more than I've ever imagined."

— Isabel Donadio-Fagan, *Top Talent Magazine*

"Doria has brilliantly captured profound principles that we all learned during the pioneering of the Human Potential Movement: the nature of abundance, sufficiency, leverage and personal power."

— Marcia Martin, CEO and Author, *Human Potential Movement Pioneer*

"This is a book you will read and re-read because it is written by someone who actually put the principles to use, you know you can get results!"

— Dr. Letitia Wright, CEO *The Wright Place*

"This book as well as the Money & You approach will expand your consciousness, shift your thinking, and set you straight on a course for true wealth."

— Burke Franklin, *Business Power Tools*

"Without the keys in this book, we are prisoners. My lock suddenly unlocked, and closed doors flew open! I found myself with an abundance and continued access to cash that I'd never had before!"

— Carol Dysart, Co-founder *People Smart Enterprises, LLC*

EXCELLERATED BUSINESS SCHOOLS®

MONEY & YOU® PROGRAM

Since 1979

www.AccessToCashBook.com

ACCESS TO CASH

The New Definition of Wealth…and It's Not What You Think It Is

DAME DORIA (DC) CORDOVA

How to Create Resources and Relationships That Lead to Real Results You Can Leverage

A *Money & You*© series book

Access to Cash: The New Definition of Wealth…
and It's Not What You Think It Is

Published in the United States

Paperback ISBN 978–1–7364530–0–1
Hardback ISBN 978–1–7364312–9–0

Library of Congress Number: 2021921888

Cover design by Mitzy De Los Santos
Layout design by Michael De Hoyos, Jr.
Content curated by David T. Fagan

TOP TALENT PUBLISHING
SELF IMPROVEMENT, BUSINESS DEVELOPMENT BOOKS

www.TopTalentPublishing.com

To all who have always wanted to have the work their hearts' desire…

Work that is productive, profitable, joyous, peaceful and supports the world to work for 100 percent of humanity…

To my *mamacita*, Isabel; my sister Jacqueline; my family; my beloved Christian Mentzel; my global network; and to my loving, awesome BFF's.

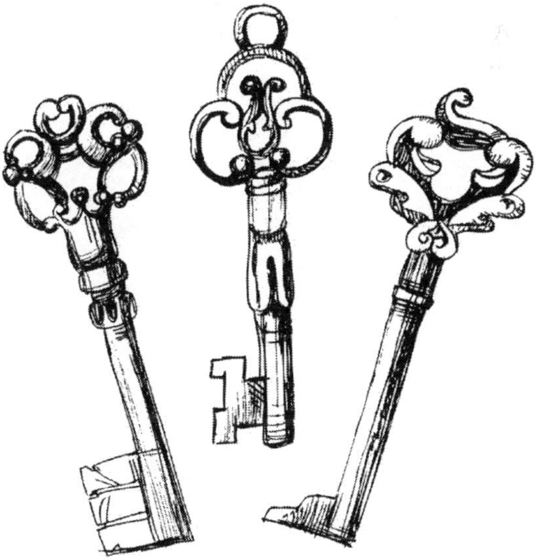

Special Thanks

To the cocreators of the work, Marshall Thurber and Bobbi DePorter, who have allowed me to have the life of my dreams…

To the many promoting partners, instructors, program directors, staff, graduates of the work from the very beginning and in all languages…

Dominique Lyone and Kerry Zurier for the decades of dedication…

To business partners/key team members through the decades, William (Bill) Galt, Pete Wanger, Greg Simmons, Robert T. Kiyosaki, Kim Kiyosaki, Andrew John Harrison, Di and John Butler, Adelene Bek, Willson Lin, Dame Wendyy Tan, Terence Tan, Jason Zeck Lee, Jacylyn Wee, Tameka Vasquez, Ryll Burgin-Doyle, Craig Doyle, Tamami Ushiki, Douglas Ng, Anne Nhi Le, Andrew Barron, Jason Estes, Jeremy Hoffmann, Tom Chesser, and others. To my teachers/mentors/masters who have influenced this work and my growth: Buckminster Fuller, Werner Erhard, Sondra Ray, Marcia Martin, Lynne Twist, Bill Galt, Carol Dysart, Dr. Cheryl Clark, Morrnah Simeona, Sai Baba, Dr. Jannie Chan (Tay), Randolph Craft, Daniel Krastins, Bill Allen, Esperanza Universall, Dr. Sananda Ananda-Maynard, Jack Canfield, Gabriel Nossovitch, Dr. Ray Blanchard, Sandra and Daniel Biskind, Jennifer Hough, and all mentors who have helped me clear "underservability" thoughts and limiting beliefs about my capabilities.

Table of Contents

Foreword

Money is a magical thing that is quite often misunderstood. Through this book you will not only crack the code of more cash in your pockets, but you will also most undoubtedly accelerate the larger ability to obtain abundance in your life.

Even though there is a growing number of financial literacy experts in the world, there is still nowhere near enough. These are the people helping others to read, speak, and translate the world of wealth on every level. The author of this book is one of the best leaders in the world when it comes to you and money, and you'll find the essence of her teachings in this book. It's no surprise that her *Money & You* program has nurtured, partnered with, taught, and been led by some of the most well-known successes of the last hundred years.

Money is something that touches all our lives very deeply, no matter who we are. So naturally, solving money challenges is the formula that is most often sought after, for when you solve the money equation, you can clear away most basic life issues to truly focus on what brings you happiness. This book is not just about access to cash; it's about access to wealth and multigenerational wealth, meaning there will be so much money that your family is taken care of for generations to come if you so choose.

Through this book you'll see the patterns, positions, and paths to good fortune that are made possible through the keys of access meant for everybody. It means wealth will no longer be limited only to those born and raised rich.

Beware of its simplicity and openness because it's tempting to cast off the lessons in this book as too good to be true. Hear my warning that the ways of this book may leave you in a state of disbelief because of how easy it can really be when you apply correct teaching to make progress with your prosperity.

Be humble, be authentic, and be thankful always.

Ken Honda

Money and happiness expert Ken Honda is a best-selling self-development author in Japan, with book sales surpassing seven million copies since 2001. His latest book is called *Happy Money: The Japanese Art of Making Peace with Your Money.*

Ken studied Law at Waseda University in Tokyo and entered the Japanese workforce as a business consultant and investor. Ken's financial expertise comes from owning and managing several businesses, including an accounting company, a management consulting firm, and a venture capital corporation. His writings bridge the topics of finance and self-help, focusing on creating and generating personal wealth and happiness through deeper self-honesty.

Ken is a philanthropist who provides ongoing support through mentoring programs, business seminars, therapeutic workshops, and correspondence courses.

Ken is the first person from Japan to be voted into the Transformational Leadership Council (TLC), a group of personal and professional development leaders, where he met Doria Cordova. He is fluent in Japanese and English; lived in Boston, Massachusetts, for two years; and currently resides in Tokyo, Japan, with his beloved family.

PART I
An Awakening to Access

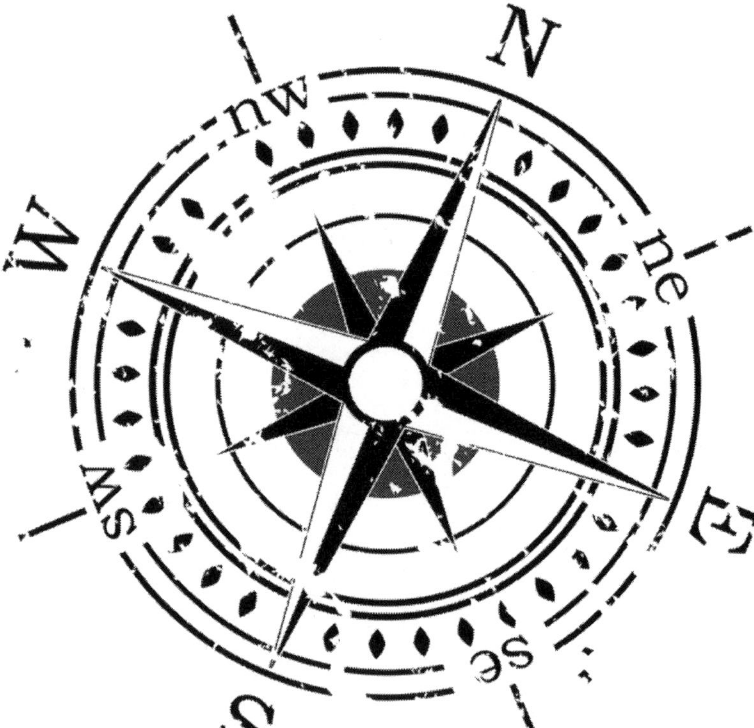
N
ne
E
se
S
sw
W
nw

The True Treasure Hunt

Direct examples of cash money are dollars, bills, or coins. This is well-known in the world.

The people that focus on this have a good chance of having some money in their lives.

Slightly indirect examples of cash money—that could be just as valuable if not more valuable—are precious metals, rare stones, stock certificates, bonds, deeds, titles, Bitcoin, or cryptocurrency. This is also somewhat known but not entirely understood.

The people that focus on this have a chance to retire or maybe even be rich.

Indirect examples of cash money are education, experts, fans, intellectual property (IP), systems, networks, and a team. This is uncommon wisdom and almost entirely misunderstood worldwide.

The people that focus on this have the greatest chance to be not just rich but to be truly prosperous and wealthy to the point that they can leave quite a lucrative legacy.

Introduction
The Prosperity Paradox

You probably think you want cash or currency in all its forms, right? If you're reading this book, you must at least have some desire to have more money in your life. Of course, the truth is that you don't want cash or money; rather, you want the things that it can provide for you, right?

As a kid, and maybe even as an adult, you probably played the genie game. It's the one where you say aloud to anyone listening what you would ask for if you were granted three wishes by a genie. If you played fair, you probably asked for all your favorite possessions like a horse, mansion, jet, sports car, or maybe even your own private island. You might have thought of something for your friends and family. You might have even asked for a life-changing miracle.

Regardless, I'm sure it didn't take long before you or someone you were playing with wished for more wishes. It's the classic move that any clever kid comes up with. Of course, we know from every Aladdin movie out there that wishing for more wishes isn't allowed, but what if it were? This book is exactly that.

What if I told you there were all kinds of genies able to grant all kinds of wishes? Stay tuned...

The truth is there are quite a few things in life that you acquire by focusing on something other than the specific thing you hope to have more of in your life. For example, you don't get more happiness and joy in your life by working for it and giving yourself every gratification you can think of at the moment.

Interestingly enough, when you spend more time giving to others, you will actually feel more happiness and joy. It's a paradox of sorts. Many times your happiness comes from making others happy. There's even a book called *Wonder Drug* by MDs Anthony Mazzarelli and Stephen Trzeciak that has scientifically proved serving others is the best medicine for you!

Time and Space

Wealth is very similar in the sense that if you think about all the direct ways to make money, you will be somewhat limited in both time and space. Yet when you focus on some of the more indirect ways to get cash—specifically, focusing on acquiring more access to wealth—things happen both easier and faster. It's the difference between addition and multiplication.

Access is the lynchpin to the law of multiplication.

If I had no cash but I have good credit, then I would have access to cash. If I had no cash, but I have access to an education, then I have access to cash. If I had no cash but had access to affluent friends, or even semi-affluent friends, I would have access to cash. If I had no cash, but I belonged to a successful network, then I have access to cash.

The Prosperity Paradox

So in a sense my focus should be on building good credit, becoming educated, attracting affluent friends, and participating in powerful network groups and other access-centric activities. This should be your focus as well if you want access to cash.

To understand and to live a life of access is to have genies with unlimited wishes at your command. It's still work, and it requires intelligence and discipline, but it's a game you can win every time. In fact, this is the handbook with all the rules of the game, including the nuances of which ones can even be bent and broken.

Chapter 1
The New Definition of Wealth

There are no poor people, only resource-poor people.
—Lynne Twist

You probably think of wealth as cash in your wallet, money in the bank, gold in the safe, or event real estate you own. Although all these things have value, there is something greater than all these, and it is extremely helpful in acquiring all of them as well.

When you chase and pursue these things that have real and perceived value, you have a decent chance of acquiring them. But if you chase the true definition of wealth, you can't help but become wealthy. What I am about to share with you is more of a law of wealth-attraction because nothing attracts more wealth than the tenet I'm about to teach you.

As one of the leaders of the entrepreneurial, experiential, transformational training industry, I have had the honor and privilege of being intimately involved with networks where these types of programs were delivered globally.

I have become friends with some of the world's leading authors, experts, and masters in business and those who have made a huge difference in the way that people relate to each other; experts who have breakthrough health technologies and distinctions, and those who can lovingly support us all in having more love, health, wealth, peace, and flexibility so that we can go through any tough situation we find ourselves in.

The Renaissance Man

I have sat at the feet of some great thinkers and masters, such as R. Buckminster "Bucky" Fuller, who was an engineer, inventor, mathematician, philosopher, author, designer, scientist, cosmogonist, new world thinker, visionary, and prophet. Bucky is considered by many to be the greatest living genius, the Leonardo DaVinci of our time, and the Benjamin Franklin of the Space Age.

He was the one who inspired me to commit to the betterment of humanity in 1977. We had the privilege of being around him until his passing on July 1, 1983, as he taught at our business schools, and we organized for him the longest program he ever taught (six days) entitled *The Future of Business.*

My Wealthy Friends

I have built global organizations with programs that have supported the stellar careers of game-changers such as Tony Robbins, Robert and Kim Kiyosaki, Jack Canfield, Mark Victor Hansen, Paul Mitchell, Ben Cohen, Bob Goldberg, and many others.

I have met world leaders like Prime Minister Mahathir of Malaysia; Fidel Castro, former leader of Cuba; ministers of education; and global change-makers like Ted Turner.

I have met billionaires who have created new industries, products, and services.

There is one thing that they all have in common: *ACCESS!*

My new definition of wealth is having access. Once you integrate this into your consciousness, your life will change. You will start to move from scarcity to sufficiency, which will ultimately take you to abundance, and nothing is sweeter because you will let go of the illusion that money will make you feel abundant and wealthy.

Wealth today means access to cash, resources, networks, investments, experts, knowledge, wisdom, support, and (these days) good medicines!

Think about all the things that you might need to build a business: competency, capital, credit, and connections, to name a few. Think of Lynne Twist's quote, "There are no poor people, only resource-poor people."

The resource-poor, the middle class, the uneducated, and those who suffer from regional disadvantage—not living in economically developed areas—don't have access to what is necessary for them to surpass their circumstances.

The rich send their children to prestigious schools for the networks they will tap into. These alumni, networks, and clubs, at their core, offer nothing more than access!

Even when I think of an extraordinary lifestyle I have been blessed to have lived for most of my adult life, I don't need to own a yacht, an airplane, a penthouse, or homes in far-away exotic places. I just need to have access to them.

Here's a great exercise for you: make a list of all that you have access to you and use as an example some of the items I listed earlier. Then make another list of what you don't have access to and go to work.

Who do you know? Who do they know? How far are you from those you need to have access to? Ask yourself, *How can I have access to those people and resources? What do I need to do? Whom do I have to meet? What networks should I be in?*

Let me give you an example.

Ted Turner

One of the people I'd always wanted to meet was Ted Turner. He was my hero for decades. He impressed me with launching CNN, creating the UN Foundation by donating $1 billion, and establishing the Goodwill Games to create harmony with Russian athletes when they were banned from the Olympics.

He earned my respect by becoming the USA's largest landowner to conserve precious land; creating the first good works cartoon hero, Captain Planet, giving children a good role model; buying and upgrading movies from Hollywood's golden age; and creating the Turner Classic Movie channel. I also loved several things in his personal life, like the fact he was married to Jane Fonda and the winner of the America's Cup.

His life partner now, who has been with him for years, is a woman I call my friend, Sally Ranney, a lifelong conservationist, environmental policy strategist, and naturalist. She serves on many for-profit and not-for-profit boards and is also president and cofounder of the American Renewable Energy Institute and the AREDAY (American Renewable Energy Day) Summit, one of the world's most prestigious and impactful environmental masterminds and educational platforms. She is a rock star in the world of conservation and renewable energy. I introduced her and her business partner, Chip Comins, to Huang Ming, the world's leading solar architect. We have aligned purposes, and we play a big game!

Should I go on about Ted Turner? If you were to Google him, you can't help being impressed. He is one of my favorite human beings, a shining example of a socially-responsible entrepreneur and a sexy rock star businessman committed to the betterment of humanity who has truly changed the world. What can I tell you? I love and admire the man!

When I first met Sally, I had no idea she was in a relationship with Ted. She is and always has been modest about that fact.

Months later we were talking, and she said, "I have to go; Ted is calling me for dinner."

I said, "Ted who?" I had no idea.

She said, "Ted, you know, my sweetie, Ted." She assumed I knew.

I repeated myself and said, "Sorry, Ted who?" And when she said Turner, I gasped.

Of course, I had to quickly share that I was a lifelong fan, had no idea they were in a romantic relationship, and how happy I was for her! She loves him deeply, and he is blessed to have her as his life partner.

When we hung up the phone, I experienced the power of accessibility so deeply.

Beyond Wealth

I felt like the wealthiest person in the world. Not that I couldn't have managed to meet him through other means. But here I had access to one of my heroes—and not because I wanted anything from him—but because whenever I can meet someone of that caliber, I will also have access to other magnificent human beings who can be partners in my missions and support me to continue on my journey of living a purpose-driven life with a million others who are also committed to making the world work for 100 percent of humanity.

When I was in Paris in December 2015 to celebrate and support the signing of the Paris Climate Accords along with many others, I met Ted and thought I had died and gone to heaven.

My new definition of wealth is truly about having access.

Money solves money problems, but no matter how much money you have, you will continue to have problems. When you reach financial abundance, you will then have what I call rich-people problems!

So you might as well go for being a peaceful, joyous, generous, and loving human being who cares for others. In the process you can create and amass great wealth for yourself, your family, your community, and the world.

And it can all happen when you truly understand access.

May the force (of access) be with you!

Chapter 2
The Car Accident

My fiancé died when I was eighteen years old. A few months later I had a miscarriage on his birthday. It was because of those horrific experiences that I dismissed the belief in a higher power. I even disdained it due to the great, heartbreaking losses I suffered. It wasn't until eight years later that my heart started to reopen, and I began searching for my purpose.

During those eight years, I personally wandered while professionally growing. I was a court reporter with a front-row view of the misery in our society. I took testimony in cases about burglaries, solicitations of sexual favors, divorces, and other matters. It wasn't unusual for me to see pimps in big fur coats with outrageous hats stroll into court with their lady workers hanging all over them. It was a bit ridiculous and very intense for a young person like me to experience the dark side of life.

I learned a lot about the way the world worked legally and illegally. I made great money, and my friends and I competed to see who could spend the most taking each other on vacations. This included three-day parties with live bands and all the goodies that came with that scene. It was a blast but boring after a while. Several ideas to cure my boredom included going to law school or starting over somewhere new. I went with moving to Hawaii.

Soul Searching

I went in search of meaning, although I don't think I knew that at the time. I was still making great money because I was a well-paid professional. I worked very hard at being successful. I was diligent and thrived in many ways.

Then it all changed with an experience of enlightenment.

I got my marching orders from the Big Guy upstairs during an out-of-body experience where I did not hear but rather sensed a message: *You were not put on this earth to be a party girl; you have a job to do.*

I ultimately learned I was destined to integrate my past legal career with the teachings of Bucky Fuller, then attend the first business school of its kind, taught by many masters two years after my enlightenment experience. That was when my real education began. It enhanced my mind and fed my soul.

In addition, during this time in the '70s, there was a whole movement about raising your prosperity consciousness. The topic had been covered by great wealth thinkers like Napoleon Hill (*Think and Grow Rich*), Wallace D. Wattles (*Science of Getting Rich*), Norman Vincent Peale (*The Power of Positive Thinking*), and James Allen (*As a Man Thinketh*). My close personal favorite of this genre is Catherine Ponder's *The Dynamic Laws of Prosperity.* Access to these trendsetters—considered new thinkers back then—and their teachings was nothing less than transformational.

Before Computers

You must remember that during that day and age, you didn't have the Internet, YouTube, or social media to hear these thought leaders. It was by word of mouth, reading, studying, and traveling to seminars and conventions to experience as much as you could, sitting in an audience listening.

One of these new thinkers was Reverend Ike, a Baptist preacher who started the most outrageous conversations about people's *deservability* of money. He often made people upset, saying things like: *It's easier to enjoy money in the back of a Rolls Royce* or *I'm not Black; I'm green like money.*

One of my favorites, which we still use to this day in our *Money & You* program, is: *You can go to the ocean of abundance with a tractor-trailer or a spoon. The ocean doesn't care. The ocean just wants to outflow.*

This kind of thinking—of being—is the way to be truly wealthy and prosperous. It's not a natural way of seeing the world nor an education you can easily find even today. It was, and still is, the access to these individuals and their teachings that helped me attract true lasting wealth. When you subscribe to these advanced ways of thinking, when my or others' wealth subsides or dips, we always have the blueprint for bringing it back.

My Kids

I never had my own children, but I have loved many. I've lived a life of service; children everywhere are my kids. I have made it my life's work to cure the world of hunger, a mission that

I still strive for today. Chris Mentzel is my beloved partner as I am starting to move into the legacy stage of my life, and happily, I have four bonus grandchildren through him.

From partying to purpose and from disbelief to a relationship with the Divine, I have been a Ho'oponopono practitioner since 1984. For me, access to a higher power is paramount and my secret weapon to success!

The Car Accident

Chapter 3
Access Points

You, like most, probably don't even understand all the access you have in your life now as well as the smaller points that lead to some of the bigger points of access. There are many points of access to cash as well as subpoints of that access! The most powerful points are often hanging in plain sight.

An example of an access point is education, and an example of a subpoint is the Internet. The Internet, if used correctly, can provide quite a significant education, and that knowledge and wisdom can give you access to cash.

Another example of an access point is credit, and an example of a subpoint is a credit card. Credit cards, if used correctly, can contribute to a strong credit score or standing that can ultimately give you access to cash.

Yet one more example of an access point is networks, and an example of a subpoint is a connection. Connections that know who and what you need to know can be a powerful part of your larger network that can lead to cash. Here is a quiz to help you locate the points of access or even subpoints of access in your current world.

Access to Cash Self-Assessment Test

What's Your Grade?

Grade how true these twenty statements are for you on a scale of 1–5: 1) never or no; 2) almost never or not really; 3) sometimes or sort of; 4) almost always or above average amount; 5) always or yes, I do this really well.

- I know people of influence and affluence.
- People of influence and affluence know me.
- I have relationships with people in the media.
- I am friends with people who facilitate events.
- I am open to strategic partnerships, joint ventures, and masterminds.
- I'm always developing my skills and talents.
- I work hard to pay people as promised.
- I use credit enough to have good credit.
- I understand how to have a good credit score.
- I am an avid reader of wisdom-filled articles and books.
- I am good at research and can be self-taught.
- I obtain and maintain investments that are most likely to grow.
- I diversify my investments.
- I keep my word with others.
- I participate in relevant and meaningful workshops and seminars.
- I believe prosperity is possible.
- I believe money is everywhere.
- I attract the help I need to grow.

- I am surrounded by people who completely support my financial success.
- I know my money psychology.

These questions are based on your ability to leverage an ongoing education, good credit, valuable relationships, true investments, and money mindsets, which are some of the cornerstones of access to cash. There are plenty more questions that can work to help you better understand what you already have around you, as well as what you still need more prevalent in your life.

Here's another way to look at the cornerstones, or five pillars, of prosperity, in terms of accelerating your access to cash—and notice that some overlap or connect.

The education access point includes things like the subpoints of social media, websites, podcasts, programs, seminars, general schools, various academies, accredited universities, trade schools, and mentors.

Credit access points include things like the subpoints of lines of credit, credit cards, auto loans, school loans, home loans, business loans, venture capital, and government grants.

Relationships are access points that include things like the subpoints of friends, family, coworkers, neighbors, classmates, teammates, peers, apprentices, mentors, teachers, networks, and people in proximity.

Investments are access points that include things like the subpoints of precious metals, stocks, bonds, real estate, cryptocurrency, education, mentorships, and relationships.

Mindsets are access points that include subpoints of awareness, affirmations, universal truths, the power of positivity, visualization, calm under pressure, emotional intelligence, inner strength, and the pursuit of success habits.

Did you see when the access points connected and overlapped? I hope so! And by this point after reading all this, you can't help but be impacted so that you are now considering and reconsidering what you value, prioritize, and worship most in your life. That is the path to true and lasting empowerment.

This new awareness starts with an audit of your life. This chapter helped you more consciously recognize what you have in abundance, as well as what is absent when it comes to your ability to access cash and, ultimately, wealth.

Still, there is something beyond wealth, and it's the root word of empowerment: power.

Chapter 4
Fulcrums and Pulleys

The real title to this book might just be *Access to Power*. This *Access to Cash* book is an instrumental part of my *Money & You* series, but the words *cash* and *money* are more about the marketing or packaging of the valuable wisdom I'm sharing than they are the literal goals of what's being taught. If you haven't already realized this, sooner rather than later you will see that things like cash and money are nothing more than an exchange of energy and a means to an end.

You have wants and needs that can be too heavy to lift; you need a lever to lighten the load. This lever can also be referred to as leverage. The piece or triangle that you press the lever against is the fulcrum. This fulcrum is your access or access point.

The same can be said of a pulley that plays the same role as the fulcrum, giving you leverage that ultimately lightens the load of the things you most want to lift into your life.

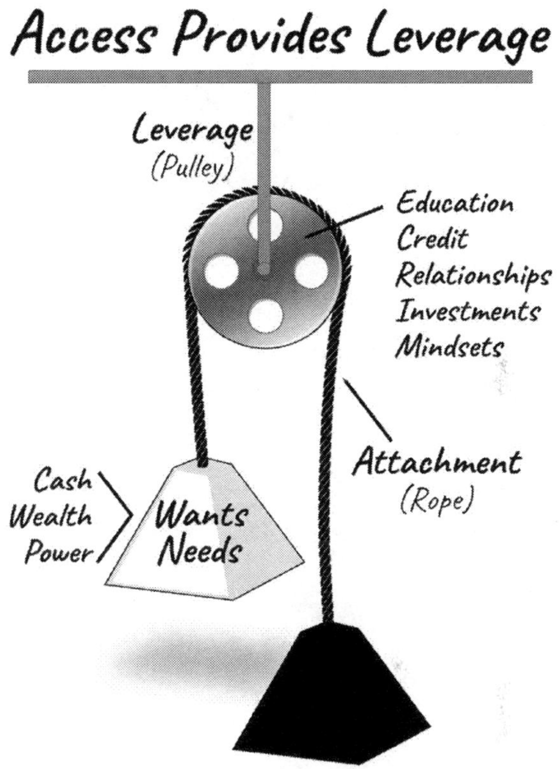

Crooked Nail

Have you ever tried to pull a crooked nail partly pounded into a piece of wood out with your fingers? It's extremely difficult, if not impossible. Yet, if you had the right tool, say a hammer, you could use the backend claw at the top to get under the head of the nail and then use the leverage of the long handle to lift that same nail up and out with a fraction of the effort.

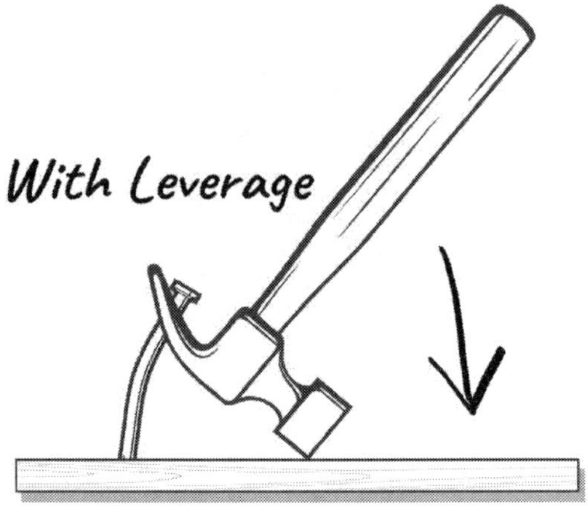

Interestingly, even using a hammer to drive a nail into something is also using leverage. The longer the handle, the more leverage, weight, and momentum that are harnessed to hammer the nail through. At first a long-handled hammer might be tough to hold and control. That's why many who first start using a hammer put their hand halfway up the handle.

It can take practice to swing on target with the full force the hammer is capable of, but with experience comes more leverage with less effort. The same can be said of all types of access points and subpoints. These things take practice, coordination, and strength of all kinds.

Understanding leverage, having the right tools, and knowing how to use them, can save time, money, and all types of pain. To have cash, wealth, and power is to have access to fulcrums and pulleys that provide leverage to lift the heavy things in life with ease.

PART II
The Five Points of Access

Chapter 5
Hair Salons and Courtrooms

Education is the highest form of leverage.
—Marshall Thurber

Before we moved to the United States, my mother owned a hair salon that ran out of a shopping mall in a prestigious area of downtown Santiago, Chile. Sometimes after school and on most Saturdays, I could be found there helping by doing things like running the cash register. My money training started early!

Being a hard worker is in my DNA, as is being a business owner, a delegator, and a person of leverage. My mother leveraged her shop to bring in other hairdressers to pay rent. She leveraged her business brand to attract clients for both her and her subcontractors.

My education consisted of traditional schooling but also trade school for court reporting, business school curricula, programs in just about every area of running a successful business, seminars, conferences, being mentored by some of the world's leading entrepreneurs, and more.

Although everyone needs some education, not everyone needs the same education. Nor does everyone learn the same way.

It's for those reasons that I encourage people to customize their education and seek the learning experience that best serves them.

Still in the Game

Today I still push myself to learn by participating in workshops, masterminds, coursework, and mentorships. I continually surround myself with people who are experts at every level. This allows me to not only learn but to keep my finger on the pulse of the overall progress of education and how fast as a society we are solving major problems in this world.

This type of continuous learning has helped me to not only know the trends but also to see them before they happen and to be a trendsetter myself.

Knowledge has never been easier to find, but it's finding the best way to absorb and implement the knowledge that proves the most difficult. Having resources that give you the best answers in the shortest amount of time is really what proves to be most valuable.

Searching for a topic online can be an easy way to get information, but then searching your findings can be work in and of itself; thus, when you find the people and resources you need most, hang on to them! My educational journey is filled with great tools, systems, and technologies.

I Like Colors

I'm a big note-taker and a huge proponent of mind mapping, a detailed and stylized note-taking system that we originally learned from one of the masters, Tony Buzan, in 1978! At our live events, you will receive a binder of preorganized blank papers and colored markers to enhance your learning experience. I have notes going back decades. I also know that my students still have many of the notes they have taken in our programs. Some have kept their program evaluation review technique (PERT) charts that they created along with their to-dos written on Post-it notes, placing them on big posters and flip chart sheets to create their dream business or organizations.

The fact of the matter is you need to know your personal learning style; to do so is to take responsibility for your education. No one is more responsible than you for your knowledge and wisdom. This is more than just being an adult; it's being a prosperous individual capable of creating extraordinary results.

There are many ways to learn, and depending on how you break things down or build things out, you might see as many as seven of them. Let's focus on the top three.

Top Three Ways to Learn

Visual: A person who does best when learning by seeing things like pictures, images, diagrams, and boards.

Auditory: A person who does best when learning by hearing – that could involve rhythm, sounds, music, or a voice

Kinesthetic: A person who does best by doing via physical activities like hands-on participation.

Again, these can be broken down into more details, but this is the core of the learning styles you need to know to absorb as much knowledge and wisdom as possible.

If you can learn easily through any one of these learning styles, you have a distinct advantage as a student and are most likely to succeed in traditional schools—as long as you can stay focused. Your attention span is also an important part of your ability to learn effectively.

Here are some of my favorite ways to stay present when learning any subject:

- Make the decision that you are going to allow the teachers, trainers, or speakers to add value to your life. Mentally fighting the information you're presented with will prevent you from getting the most out of any learning situation.
- Put away distractions like your phone.
- Ask questions whenever you can.
- Take notes in creative ways.
- Take occasional breaks to stay fresh.
- Enter learning sessions well-rested.
- Stay hydrated.
- Eat for energy.
- Review the materials as soon as you can by sharing what you learned or discussing the teachings with your partner, team, or friends.

When we teach in our programs, workshops, and events, we not only utilize the three main modalities that people learn through, but we also help them by providing the environment to support the nine recommendations listed above.

Street Smarts

As someone who spent years inside courtrooms listening to, viewing, translating, and taking down testimony, I witnessed a lot that gave me quite the education. I learned about law, justice, life, misery, and love. I had a front-row view of judgments, sentencing, heartbreak, and hope. It was a unique experience that served me well, and we all have the ability to get involved in the world around us and become a student of life.

Education is everywhere for all of us. Of course, there are places in this world where access to education proves very difficult. You can change that, be that conduit, but it requires you to educate yourself. Do not take your accessibility to ongoing education for granted. It is one of the keys to success because it leads to access cash and abundance.

Chapter 6
Cards and Loans

This can make you or break you. It is potentially the most dangerous of all the five pillars of access. None of the other four pillars has as much of a downside as this one. If your relationship with money is weak or flawed, the destruction and bondage you can find yourself in are like no other in today's modern era.

Still, if you can master this book and its teachings completely, then this is a game-changer. One key to this is understanding what appreciating assets are—physical things that increase in value—and which ones are more likely to go up over time. Assets like established businesses with duplicatable systems (and automation), IP, good teams, and a great reputation are most likely to stand the test of time.

Many times the mistakes we make using credit are from thinking that because we have something to show for our money, it means that we made a wise purchase. That simply isn't the case. Buying and owning things can require insurance, maintenance, storage, fuel, energy, time, and stress beyond measure.

Plus, many of the physical things we buy are depreciating assets, meaning that their value is more likely to go down over time.

Access is always tied to leverage, so it's no surprise that, once again, the point being made is that leveraging your credit standing can give you access to loans. This access can allow you to leverage assets that you can grow and further leverage to access even more cash and assets.

I have done this many times with different assets. Through the decades I have been able to leverage my assets to finance my business, invest in businesses that are in alignment with my purpose, and get involved with new technologies.

Mr. Rich Dad Himself

My past partner of nine years, the coauthor of the *Rich Dad Poor Dad* series, Robert Kiyosaki, fell in love with leverage when he first understood its depth and importance after he attended and later taught our signature programs, *Money & You*, our Excellerated Business School for Entrepreneurs, and other Excellerated programs. He developed a powerful, genius-like ability when it came to leveraging and access. The key was made, and the doors it opened were nothing less than access and abundance at the most advanced levels.

Speaking of access, Robert's next business partner after me was Sharon Lechter, who is second to none in the world of financial literacy and another master of leverage. Along with her brilliant lawyer husband, Michael, they opened doors for publishing and marketing resources (and much more) for Robert that he could only have dreamed of. I don't think the *Rich Dad* series would have been the colossal success it was without her involvement.

And had he not met her, I wouldn't have had one of my

dreams come true: to be a part of a *Think and Grow Rich* book. When she invited me to be a contributor for the women's version of the book, I thought I had died and gone to heaven—access is powerful!

In the seventeen years that Robert and I were in each other's lives, we created dreams together for him to be as famous and successful as he became and for my work to expand globally, as it continues to do.

Credit is like a diamond: it has many facets. Credit at its core is nothing more than the belief you create in others that you are a worthy risk to lend money or provide resources to—for them to get behind your dreams. You establish that good standing by keeping agreements that you made, particularly for loan terms and meeting those terms on time.

One Way to Go

It's best to start small and proceed with caution. For many people around the world, this can include secured credit cards where you give the bank money, and then they allow you to borrow against that amount and make payments on whatever you borrow. Establishing your ability to pay back on time will prove that you are worthy of receiving unsecured credit cards based on your on-time payment history, income, debts, and stability of job and residence.

It's also best to use your cards for things you would normally purchase, like gas for a vehicle or food for your fridge. There are plenty of good credit-building tips that many of our expert graduates can share with you or that you can find online. The overall concept is to go slow, know what the true costs of interest are, what the difference is between depreciating assets and appreciating assets, and what's best to leverage with credit.

Another good tool is arbitrage (financing), which is your ability to make more money than the money costs you. For example, if you can make 12 percent interest in the stock market and it only costs you 6 percent to borrow, you've successfully made more than it costs you, which is arbitrage at its most basic level.

Another example: if it costs you $5,000 to borrow $50,000 for a down payment on a house for $50,000 less than it's worth and resell it for a profit of $35,000, you have a net profit increase of $30,000. That once again is leverage, access, and making money with other people's money, which is also a form of arbitrage in this case.

And now you have a whole new world of cryptocurrency, which brings with it another avenue for credit and borrowing against crypto that may be held in one of the many secure platforms that makes it easy to buy, sell, and store Bitcoin, Ethereum, and other cryptocurrencies.

I'd even go so far as to say that this new trend is taking a rightful place next to gold, real estate, and other more traditional assets. Otherwise, governments internationally would not be passing regulations, laws, and guidelines to regulate their use.

It's good to be diversified, and I am an entrepreneurial animal. I learned from the masters, like Jay Abraham, that your greatest wealth can come from your own business, so why not use credit to finance your endeavors?

The reverse might also be true: although it's good to have money saved up in various kinds of accounts for a rainy day, if that money is only making you a rate of return of less than 1 percent or even 0 percent, it would be better for you to pay off credit cards balances that are at rates of 15 percent to 30 percent.

Playing the Game

Credit is a game in and of itself. There is the personal credit game as well as the business credit game. This shouldn't be confused with school loans or even government grants, but regardless there is a lot of money to be leveraged out there. Even friends and family have been a source of many startups' seed money and investments of all kinds. The additional potential risks and interpersonal problems with that should be obvious, but it is another way to go.

Even in these personal settings with friends and family members, your reputation for keeping your word and repaying your commitment on time, over time, is a factor for sure. Use credit as a leverage tool, not a tool that will bury you alive!

The Billion-Dollar Business

Nowadays, there are credit monitoring, building, and reporting services because it affects so much of our lives. There's a plethora of books and courses just on credit itself.

When you understand it and can leverage it, whole new worlds are opened to you. I know people who have made millions with little to no money of their own by using credit to leverage appreciating assets.

You don't need cash when you have credit to access and unlock other opportunities. It's an almost unmatched tool although just because you have credit doesn't mean it's the best tool to leverage in every situation.

Chapter 7
Bucky the Beautiful

You might have heard that you are the average of the success and wealth of the five people you spend the most time with. There are many versions of this saying, and it is truer than not. I believe this can also include the people we read and study. Meaning that if you've studied Gandhi, Buddha, Allah, or Jesus weekly or daily, these masters could have an impact on your state of being as if they were one of the five people you spend time with.

One of the people in my life that qualifies as one of my top five influencers and mentors is Bucky Fuller. He is known as the planet's friendly genius and is perhaps one of the best-known American thinkers of the last century.

He developed the World Game—its essence is heavily covered in our *Money & You* program—as well as his mathematics known as synergetics. He also created the geodesic dome and was recognized globally for his creative contributions to technology and the future. Some consider him the Leonardo DaVinci of our time. Many of the principles we teach in our programs come from him. Knowing and working with him, even being a student of his teachings, is access to the Divine and the mega-mind inside all of us.

The relationships we have through face-to-face conversations (and communication devices) connect us around the world; even teachings that originated in the past can have a special meaning in our lives. They can be inspiring, enlightening, and empowering.

In the Flesh

I have enjoyed many powerful face-to-face conversations over the decades that include the brilliance of Bucky Fuller, Werner Erhard, Marshall Thurber, Tony Robbins, Bill Galt, Jack Canfield, Mark Victor Hansen, Robert and Kim Kiyosaki, Dominique Lyone, Dr. Jannie Tay, Sharon Lechter, Keith Cunningham, Dolf de Roos, John Gray, Dr. Ivan Meisner, Lynne Twist, Kerry Zurier, Willson Lin, Bill Allen, Joel Seiden, Ken Honda, Maria Simone, Chad Warren, Sally Ranney, Roger Salam, David T. Fagan, Tony Nash, Moe Rock, Forbes Riley, Dr. Finance, and Diamond Diva to name just a few business and transformational leaders.

These people have been resources to me in the past, are in the present, and will be in the future. They are a resource through the phone or even through my memories of them that I have well documented. I have had the privilege and honor of being around some of the world's greatest minds, even during their greatest accomplishments. I don't mention this to take credit for what they achieved but rather to pay homage to the power of personal relationships.

The Golden Rolodex

Who are you seeking out? Who can you call a friend that you can call on for support and advice? Building your Rolodex, your network, and a mastermind of beautiful souls and brilliant minds should be a critical mission on your road to riches. I treasure all my relationships made on the path to sufficiency, which have allowed me to experience abundance. It has allowed me to feed the world in more ways than one.

People are key to some of the other pillars of access. People can be a part of your educational journey, your credit capabilities, manifest your mindset, and can also be the best investment you can make. Look for the people who bring out the best in you. Search for the people who are givers more than takers and be willing to invest in them as well. Be humble, be teachable, be a friend, and serve them well. Make sure you fill your relationship "bank account" with many more deposits than withdrawals.

Don't try to be the smartest person in the room; look for the places where you will learn the most. Avoid being defensive or having an attitude of knowing everything. The words *I know* are the enemy of learning. I like my mentor Marshall Thurber's purpose: love, learn, and earn, which summarizes it best!

I have developed relationships for decades. I have favors I could call in all over the planet. If I were ever out of money, there are at least 100 people I know that would give me $1,000 with no strings attached. Add it up; that's $100,000! That is just one more way of demonstrating the power of the Access to Cash belief system.

David T. Fagan, another friend of mine, teaches the value of high-dollar, low-maintenance friendships. This isn't to say you only associate with people that can help you in some strategic monetary way, but it is to say that when you are building your network, you must continually level up to the best people.

Friends with Those Gone

Bucky is a beautiful being who is still my friend—and to many others—through the teachings he left for us to study and apply in our daily lives and businesses. Many of the great minds we have lost have done the same.

People have always been my greatest asset, and the source I invest the most in. I might even say that I use leverage through giving them some valuable exchange, paying for their time, or sharing the wealth. My business has almost exclusively grown because of the good people who have been attracted to support our purpose and missions. Together we continually create profitable endeavors.

Chapter 8
Gold Coins, Bitcoin, and Businesses

Your income typically comes before any significant investments that you may have made, and some you invest first and then make money. This includes investing in your education, building your credit, and in your relationships. Still, the larger idea in this chapter is based more on the greatest appreciating assets you'll want to consider leveraging so that you have greater access to cash.

Over the years I have mostly invested in my businesses, others' dreams, and awesome products and services. More recently I have been educating myself in the world of cryptocurrency—the future of global monetary exchanges, both big and small. I have also invested in precious metals, the stock market, and various streams of income through the world of network marketing. My interest in a variety of investments has allowed me to build a diversified portfolio.

You need to control and leverage an asset that can grow in value because, as they do, they can give you access to more wealth, including cash.

Many have the ability for homeownership, which has a mortgage payment almost equal to—if not lesser than—what they would pay for rent. As their house goes up in value, the equity in that home can be leveraged through a relatively low-interest home equity loan. At times this does not require extra money; it's just money used differently, which is just another way of saying that investment can lead to access to cash.

Everything from self-directed IRAs to cryptocurrency like Bitcoin is just money used more efficiently. Time plays a factor as well, so you might say that true access to cash is time and money used more efficiently for exponential growth.

Time Savers

Think about the time it takes to do certain things in your life and ask if there is something that you might invest in to save your valuable time. It is common knowledge in many schools of thought and business that we should delegate tasks that are drastically fewer-dollar jobs. If your time is worth $150 an hour, consider delegating the jobs that can be done for $30 an hour. With that being said, some people don't understand the value of their time, making the mistake of assuming it is less than or more than it is.

Money Mistakes

Another common mistake is thinking and saying: *This investment will pay for itself.* Many times people spend money on office space, equipment, technology, and hiring people too soon, taking on too much debt, and not understanding its true costs. Most companies fail in the first couple of years because of these mistakes

Plus, people also pay themselves too much, too fast. I prefer to use the rule of thirds that says to invest one-third in a safe area, one-third in medium-risk investments that might bring bigger returns, and last, one-third in high-risk investments that might bring the highest returns, but your financial security is not at risk if you lose it.

Still, you might only be investing a small part of what you have access to. The biggest and best investment you can make as a business owner is in your own business. That doesn't mean you don't invest in other things; it just means your business should be a big part of the investment slice of your money pie.

The more money you make, the more you will be required to learn about money and investing. You need to learn how to use it, spend it, invest it, and ultimately leverage it. Do not leave it up to accountants, financial planners, bankers, attorneys, or anyone other than you. Be willing to be 100 percent responsible for your money.

To have control over it, you must own the process of investing. That doesn't mean that you don't seek out trusted advisers to provide you with educated options; it just means the buck stops with you.

Here's where I always recommend that you become familiar with my old partner's book, *The Cashflow Quadrant*, which was taught to us back in 1991 by a financial master, Keith Cunningham, an Excellerated Business School instructor. Be clear on the quadrant or what lane you are making your money in.

Investing has its own rules. I always say that if you are not willing to become a full-time student of the subject, you are most likely going to have some tough learning experiences. Invest as you would build a business. Many of the same rules apply!

A Second Full-Time Job

There may come a time when it feels like a full-time job to manage your own money, and you must prepare yourself emotionally—and systems-wise—to make large amounts of money. If you expect magic, do it based on solid wealth-building principles.

As simple as it may sound, buying low, selling high, and leveraging everything in between is still good advice!

For those of you who have a business, you can also be tempted to overfund and invest in it. Buying a home or other properties can be a good investment, provided that long term it gives you meaningful tax deductions and equity that can be leveraged later. Paying off high-interest credit cards and freeing up more money per month to put back into your business is also a great step.

You must become a lifelong student of money, taxes, investments, and business to reach the greatest height of wealth and abundance. Look at your investments as vehicles that can help you achieve the goals of stability, passive residual income, money-making-money, and overall financial freedom.

You'll want to own, control, and leverage these various vehicles to get you to your dreams.

Chapter 9
Affirmations, Mantras, and Manifestos

You probably think that the last pillar of mindset is the first thing you should focus on. I chose to make it last so you remember it most. What I learned most from people who are very successful—in every area of their lives—is the power of the mind. And what I have learned from the most affluent and influential people in my life is the power of accessibility and connections. I have done a lot of work to remove the negative beliefs, decisions, and voices in my head and enhance the positive ones about money, success, and having a positive impact on the world.

Your money story, as well as all the stories being told inside your head, need to be addressed, dealt with, and rewritten as needed for you to be the best version of yourself and the best decision maker you can be.

After all, every decision you have ever made has led you exactly to where you are today. We've been told: *If you want to be in a better place, then you must make better decisions.* Most, if not all, of your bad money decisions, come from the limiting beliefs living inside you.

Daily disciplines like Transcendental Meditation (TM) are extremely beneficial. TM has been a part of my daily routine for twelve years as of this writing. I learned this invaluable practice from Dr. Sananda. It was through her skillful mentoring that I learned even more distinctions on how to meet any challenge that may come up in my life. Thanks to her and several other spiritual mentors I've had in my life, I face challenges with mastery, clarity, and great love.

I block off a couple of hours every morning to start my day right, and I easily outwork people half my age because of my routines, disciplines, and rituals. My mantras make a difference. I do my best not to worship long hours; instead, I prioritize income-generating activities, creating leverage, and having productive and meaningful days.

Always be careful with what you say because your mind is always eavesdropping. It's common for me at events to interrupt those who are expressing limiting beliefs about themselves so that the universe might be even more rigged in their favor.

Some of my favorite affirmations are:

This too shall pass.

I am successful.

I am confident.

All I need is within me right now.

I am the hero of my own story.

Today is going to be a good day.

I am loved, and I choose to love others.

I am independent and self-sufficient.

I am living within sufficiency, which leads me to great abundance.

I am grateful for all that I have.

My soul radiates and warms the souls of others.

I will lift up and love everyone I talk with today.

I finish what matters and let go of what does not.

Happiness is a choice, and today I choose to be happy.

I free myself from all destructive doubt.

Our inner voice and outer voice must say in unison with these positive words of affirmation to accelerate our best decision-making abilities. This is fundamental to financial abundance. These mindsets lead to access to cash and so much more. Words are the keys to so many methods that attract money.

The opposite of abundance is scarcity, so we must speak internally and externally without short-sighted thoughts and ideas. Beware of words that limit you or others. Negative words should be treated like the true curse words they are; they can hex you from the sweet honey of life.

Some of the curse word phrases include:

I'm broke. You are not broke; you are just temporarily out of cash.

I'm an idiot. You are never an idiot, even though you may have temporarily acted like one.

Why can't I be like them? Instead, say: *They are very good, and I can be very good too.*

It's all my fault. It is rarely all your fault, and even when it is, it's better to say: *I played a part in the situation, and I am only responsible for my own decisions and actions.*

I'm a failure. Failure is an event, not a person. Instead, say: *I will learn from this.*

I'll never get this. It may not even be important for you to get something, so instead, say: *I will get this in my own time and way, and I will learn everything I can from the process.*

I'm not good enough. This is never true. We are all good enough in our own way. Instead, say: *Even if I'm not good at this, I know I'm good at plenty of things. I must find those talents, or I was born good enough for this world.*

I wish I didn't have such bad luck. True lasting success isn't about luck; it's preparation plus opportunity that most often creates success. Instead, say: *I am in control of my own destiny.*

It's too late for me, so why try? It's rarely too late for you, and there is always something new to try. Experiment with the words like: *Today is a new day, and I have learned from yesterday.*

I don't have the money. Many times it is not about the number of our resources; it's often about our resourcefulness. Instead, say: *Money and opportunities for resources are everywhere.*

The things we say to ourselves, inside and aloud, must be constantly monitored and manipulated for our own good. These internal conversations are directly linked to the mindset that keeps us close to the money that leads to the wealth that can change the world forever. Some of my most influential and well-known friends have built their empires around the ability to constantly grow and master their wealth mindset. I'll never forget my first meeting with Tony Robbins in the early '80s and later, putting him on a plane to Hawaii for one of his first big Firewalk events for our *Money & You* network.

Even then his ability reflected a natural talent for inner work. Through the decades he has refined his message mindset and has changed the lives of millions with that message. I love being a part of the team that created his first organization. I can say the same about Robert and Kim Kiyosaki. Being there at the start of their work in the training industry is something I will remember until the day I leave this beautiful world and into the Great Beyond. Being part of changing the world is an unforgettable experience!

Whether the teachings are from our world-renowned *Money & You* program or our Excellerated Business School, mindset is always at the core. Our training is all mind and consciousness-centric. My greatest heroes are those who have mastered their minds and have found their true north in their hearts.

PART III
Money-Making Activities

Chapter 10
From Ditch Diggers to Doctors

Although you might make more money in one job over another, all work has value. Some people identify with what they do for work, but what you do to make money should not define you as a human being. Still, you may love a job that doesn't yield a high hourly rate of pay.

The rewards may be elsewhere for many that do the jobs we all need done to make this world go around.

I worked a job for a few years, and it provided me with many things. Regardless of your career, it's not how much money you make; it's how much you can save and invest. It's not about your hourly rate that ultimately dictates your access to cash; it's how you use whatever money you have. I know many millionaires that act as if they have no money: living below their means, saving continually, and investing wisely. Ronald Read, a retired janitor in Vermont, amassed a fortune of $8 million from smart spending and investing habits over a long period.

A friend and neighbor, Mark Richards, was quoted as saying, "I'm sure if he earned $50 a week, he probably invested $40 of it."

The *Wall Street Journal* reported that at the time of his death, Read had at least ninety-five stocks, many of which he had for years—if not decades. The point is that not having a job—nor the type of job you have—can stop you from amassing great wealth, let alone keep you from having access to cash.

Buy Back Your Life

There is more to life than working. More and more people are buying back their lives by learning to live on less and creating more time to enjoy their own personal pursuits, hobbies, and interests. Happiness does not have to come from the workplace, and a truly happy person knows they are their own source of joy. It's one's attitude toward a job that creates happiness more than anything else.

This isn't to say you shouldn't find a job you truly enjoy; it's just to say that a job isn't the end-all of existing. It does not define you, nor does it limit your ability to have abundance in your life. It's often the journey of some jobs that ultimately lead many to figure out what they truly want to do or even what matters most in their lives.

It might surprise you to know that the rate of pay isn't even what employees care the most about in their jobs. According to the *Washington Post*, when choosing a career, personal fulfillment is at the top of the list, and I would have to agree with that. Choose a job that is fulfilling to you, provides room to grow, and is something you can do day in and day out. Maybe you value working from home, or maybe you like the benefits or perks they offer.

If you want to rise through the ranks of most companies so that you can take on more responsibility and make more money, that is a worthy pursuit as well.

Here are ten things anyone can do to be successful at their job:

- be on time
- be teachable
- be hardworking
- be prepared
- be passionate
- be consistent
- be a connector
- have high energy
- have a good attitude
- do more than expected

The bottom line is that a lot of this has to do with self-respect. When you do a good job, you get results; do all the things on my top ten list and you'll earn the respect of others.

People who are respected get opportunities to share their opinion, make decisions, and have more responsibilities. Still, if you are good at something, make sure you are paid the most possible for that skill. Adopting my top ten list will only take you so far. For example, you could be the best salesperson in the world, but if you are selling hot dogs, unless you own a franchise, you will most likely not make as much as someone selling houses, businesses, or having a licensing model like I do.

Also, don't forget to know all the things your employer provides and their associated value. There are companies that will pay for some, if not all, of advanced schooling costs. Others will match what you contribute to your 401k or provide various performance bonuses. These things need to be ascertained because they are all opportunities to be leveraged.

Whether you work for yourself or for someone else, you should know the three stages of money: making it, keeping it, and growing it.

You must be honest with yourself as to where you are at because each stage requires different habits, education, and risks. For instance, for you to make money, you need to clarify what profession or business is best suited for your personality, skills, knowledge, and interests. Keeping it will require you to have good money habits and to know yourself well. You want to know your weaknesses, shortcomings, and strengths!

As important as a job or career is, it won't be what gets you to financial independence. To grow money you will need to be educated in the five pillars of access to cash—which can help anyone at any level obtain multigenerational wealth—as well as the expanded topics that are discussed inside these pages.

Chapter 11
Salespeople, Network Marketers, and Business Owners

You're seeing these three things in the same chapter because they are in the same category, in the sense that your income and your day-to-day activities are almost entirely up to you. You must take total ownership if you are a 100 percent commissioned salesperson, network marketing representative, or entrepreneur. That means how you choose to spend your time, your ability to be self-taught and self-directed, your ability to stay focused and take action, and your overall work ethic will matter greatly. Even though there might be people to cheer you on or even apply pressure, it is ultimately up to you to produce a profit.

If you fall into any of these categories, you will need to excel in the four major areas of business self-mastery: 1) money and finances; 2) sales and marketing; 3) people and organization; 4) and technical expertise in your industry.

A lot of thought and consideration went into these topics. Many books have been written on these subjects. The purpose of our discussion here is to focus more on the highlights that need to be known as it pertains to our focus on leverage and access to cash. Just know that leveraging the five pillars—getting and staying educated, establishing and building credit, finding and cultivating relationships, making and growing investments, and developing and mastering an emotionally intelligent mindset—will serve you well when building your business because they go hand-in-hand with growth.

As one of the big three—salesperson, marketer, or business owner—you will need to become proficient in the knowledge needed to market, sell, and fulfill at every level. This often requires at least some training in websites, social media, ads, copywriting, record keeping, contract writing, bookkeeping, interviewing, hiring, problem-solving, list-building, public speaking, and various types of industry-specific technology to name a few. Your current and ongoing education will be extremely important.

Having access to credit cards, home equity loans, student loans, and business loans—which are tax write-offs in most of the world—is also really important because it provides financial resources to survive while building your business and enables you to invest in all the inventory, tools, and technology needed to sustain and grow.

Having mentors and leaders of your industry at your disposal or as a part of your extended team can also be vital on your path to victory in business. In addition, having referral partners, joint ventures, memberships with various networking groups, and belonging to various masterminds will be important when it comes to avoiding pitfalls and earning easy wins.

Making investments both in and out of your business will lead directly and indirectly to its success. As a business owner you have to continually consider owning versus renting when it comes to buildings, equipment, and other technology. Investing, whether in things or people, will be an issue of almost constant reevaluation.

Being a salesperson, a network marketer, or a business owner means facing rejection. Hearing all the noes can be quite discouraging, so a healthy mindset is crucial in this world of results-based business.

You might think this is repetitive, and you'd be right. But it's worth echoing with different words one more time for you: if you combine the five pillars of access to cash with one of these big three categories that we have been discussing in this chapter, you have the greatest odds of reaching the highest levels of income and wealth.

Chapter 12
Easy Money

Whether you're employed or self-employed, salaried or commissioned, you should always prioritize having passive income—what I call *easy money.*

Robert Kiyosaki and I also had a special category, *sushi money*, which was extra money that came in unexpected ways or as a byproduct of some of our promotional activities. *Sushi* because excellent sushi can be expensive and a treat.

And here I have to include another VIP *Money & You* graduate, Ken Honda, one of Japan's most successful authors, publishers, and transformational leaders, who wrote a magnificent book titled *Happy Money*, which is cash made from endeavors that not only make you, your family, your team, and your business associates happy but also contribute to others.

So whether we call it easy money, sushi money, or happy money, your focus should always be on creating money through leveraging different streams of income. The definition of passive income is when you earn money with little to no effort. Examples include renting out something for more than it costs or providing memberships where people pay over and over for something that was created once.

Businesses that are built on passive income include vending machine sales, tool rentals, storage units, residential homes, commercial buildings, car rentals, apps, book sales, course sales, network marketing, and licensing of IP. Anytime you can do something once and get paid many times over, it can be quite lucrative. My *Money & You* and other Excellerated programs have been licensed all over the world, and the income generated from that comes back to me over and over, regardless of my day-to-day efforts.

This is an extremely advanced example of leverage that is a constant access to cash regardless of any future work or energy on my part. Of course, I want to improve, support, and continue to expand my programs and grow the organizations, which is always done as a team effort. But I don't necessarily have to do that personally to grow my wealth.

My platforms, programs, courses, workshops, books, products, and apps all provide income streams because I created an economic engine that included building the brand, having an excellent reputation, and having the goodwill of avid fans who recommend us to their friends, associates, and networks. As for courses, books, and other physical and online products, it was easier to duplicate them. Most of the effort went into publishing them, providing them to various people and places for distribution, and supporting continuous improvement.

The New Titans of Industry

Uber leverages drivers and their cars. Airbnb leverages homeowners and their homes. Netflix leverages filmmakers and their films. Shutterstock leverages photographers and their photos. None of these giants have to buy or maintain cars or houses or create all the content they are licensed to sell. Even Amazon, the largest retailer in the world, makes its money by selling other people's goods online without the majority of the costs of manufacturing them or having to rent, own, or maintain retail locations.

This way of doing business has always been a favorite of those who want to acquire wealth, as well as the already wealthy who want to diversify it.

You might be looking to see what you can invent, manufacture, operate, and own and not notice that many create wealth by licensing, marketing, renting, and ultimately leveraging. For decades temp agencies—and more recently, virtual assistant companies—have been leveraging human power. They might hire them out at $5–$10 an hour while paying the worker 50 percent to 95 percent of what they are receiving. This is a win-win-win and a valuable service helping employers to find contractors quickly for short-term work that might become permanent work.

Like in almost every area of life, people can be taken advantage of, and I'm a proponent of fair wages around the world. I also believe business owners should make a profit from the risks they take and the services they provide.

There can be a win-win proposition in this area, and more examples can be found in this new world of entrepreneurship. As people increasingly understand the power of accessibility of resources, cash, and support, the world is getting better.

LifeWave, NuSkin, Young Living Oils, SendOutCards

Network marketers also leverage people by building strategic teams of buyers and business builders that get a small piece of the profits that can add up to quite a bit when done right.

Real estate has been a favorite American way to leverage streams of income and benefit from assets in more ways than one. From licensing IP, trademarking, and online courses to owning laundromats, storage units, parking garages, and the like can tap you into more passive income.

This doesn't mean you won't need insurance, maintenance, oversight, equipment, and support from time to time, but it's still the best way to ultimately access more resources.

Your job—or business—could be to develop passive income for yourself or your employer. Either way, you know you have security when you're in a business with low overhead costs combined with high prices or even low prices with a high number of people purchasing.

By now you may have noticed that I'm not covering investing and the various traditional investment channels that are available in the world today, including cryptocurrency. That's only because I am not an expert in that area. I am an entrepreneurial animal, so I stay in my lane because I know that subject well. There are magnificent graduates of our programs and many friends who *are* masters in investing.

If you are around me long enough, participate in my *Fridays with Doria and Friends* global platform, watch any of the many summits and online programs, or read the many books I am featured in, you'll know I do mention some of those masters. There are strict rules in the world of investing, and we bring masters in our advanced programs to cover areas of leveraging money, resources, and people to further educate entrepreneurs.

Bottom line: look for the easy money and leverage what you can. It's the smart way to get the most for the least.

PART IV
Advanced Access

Chapter 13
More Than Money

You can keep things fairly simple with access pillars, points, and subpoints, but there is a more advanced game that some of the most powerful play. It's a game of strategy, and those who play it best have the ability to think three, four, and five moves ahead—if not more.

To use the word game may indicate a cavalier view of advanced access, but that couldn't be further from the truth about this type of power. Then again to use the word power may trigger some kind of manipulative, bad-intentioned force that also wouldn't be true in the case of this book's teachings.

It can both be fun to play this game of access and empowering in a way that requires a responsible application. It reminds me of the expression: *Where much is given, much is expected.*" Bottom line, when I want to achieve great accomplishments for the masses, it helps to understand the most likely outcomes to what and how I am leveraging people, places, and things.

It's a matter of *if this, then that*, which simply means you develop an understanding of your potential moves as well as the moves of others. These moves and countermoves could also be considered forces and counterforces at play. The people who do the most good in this world often have a great understanding of how people think, act, and ultimately make decisions. Those that become wealthy and powerful keep that wealth and power by understanding all the moving parts.

This means that sometimes getting or gaining access first starts with figuring out who or what network or organization has the wealth and power now or is the easiest for you to access. Doctors, attorneys, people that hold political office, officers of the law, teachers, professors, national journalists, and scientists with major funding are just a few of the players who could be a part of your inner and outer game.

Not only can access get you cash, wealth, and power, but it can get you even more access. Some of the world's most successful people don't stop at money or the things they can buy; they turn around and leverage their wealth for greater access.

Just look at Richard Branson, Elon Musk, and others working on the new space race. It will take more than just money to get there. Just look at Bill Gates, Mark Zuckerberg, or Jeff Bezos. They didn't stop once they were number one in their industry or field. They continue to play the game even though there's nothing more they can buy with money.

That's where strategy and the ability to predict and forecast become what I call an *access multiplier* comes into play. Although this book isn't meant to teach you the game the same as our *Money & You* programs do experientially, I still want to plant the seed for what is possible. I also want to show you where these laws of access and universal truths of leverage lead when applied correctly. If you apply some of the most basic access points and subpoints into your life, you won't be able to help but have more of what you want. Still, this is only scratching the surface of the larger forces at play and available as you learn to combine the various elements in this book.

Believe it or not, if it came down to money or access, some of the world's most successful would choose the latter. All things being equal, would you rather have money or power? Keep in mind that power can get things money can't.

The same access pillars, points, and subpoints in all their various combinations are the same moves that put people in leadership positions in companies, militaries, and at the head of countries.

Chapter 14
The Greatest Power on Earth

You should realize by now that not only is access to cash a path to better decision-making that leads to wealth, but also to a lifestyle that I call high-access living.

This happens when your regular access to cash decision-making becomes habits that happen automatically. For years now—even decades—my high-access living has happened at a subconscious level where I don't even think about it in real-time.

Daily routines and rituals that involve the five pillars of access to cash are most likely to lead you to healthy habits of high-access living. For me it happens in the way I do constant research and participate in online events, workshops, networking events, and mastermind sessions, as well as putting on my own events where I am constantly connecting with people. Of course, I also check in on my own investments as needed to create a lifestyle that happens with ease.

You need to do the same: focus on the activities that lead to purpose-driven wealth building. You can't wait to be in the mood to sell or put things off until you feel ready to learn more. You can't wait for the time to be perfect before doing your inner work.

These things need to be regularly scheduled activities until they happen without thinking about them—and even then, you need to review your efforts constantly.

I like to reward myself and celebrate my wins. I've learned not to overschedule to leave time for things to go wrong or to occasionally go past allotted time blocks so I can still get all the priorities done well.

You should never plan things back-to-back or try to work for long, continuous hours without a meaningful break. You should always rest well, sleep effectively, stay hydrated, and eat well for peak performance. You can't what I recommend try randomly here and there; you must duplicate, integrate, practice, and improve on the things I've been sharing as part of your everyday living.

In the Moment

When you stay present with your purpose long enough, your commitments will be replaced with habits, which is the most powerful force of nature that you can have in life.

Remember, there is a new definition of wealth; it starts with the things that bring access to cash but doesn't end there. Money can only buy so much. Keep in mind that money doesn't necessarily get you into the best parties, enrolled in the best schools, or appointments with the most accomplished doctors. The same five pillars that give you access to cash that leads to wealth also give you access to life-changing and life-saving opportunities.

Access is a fundamental aspect of all kinds of rewarding activities, unique experiences, and priceless moments. Access has always been a secret to success, and it will continue to be of great value in the future. Although it's never been easier to get access to information, it is continually getting harder to get access to prominent universities, renowned hospitals, top doctors, and leaders of influence

When Money Doesn't Matter

When it comes to the subjects that matter to human beings, wealth is often not enough. It can come down to the family you may have been born into, the people you know, and the unique resources you have access to.

When you have the greatest access, you have more than wealth—you have real power. It's the kind of power that only a president, prime minister, or dictator might have. These are the types of positions of power that not even money can buy, which is evident in elections and the rise of worldwide leaders everywhere. For example, sometimes the leaders of countries come into power because they have access to the media or the military. You should never underestimate the power of access. It goes beyond wealth. It may be one of the greatest connections to power on the face of the earth.

There is nothing you can't accomplish without the right amount of leverage and access.

Afterword
by David T. Fagan

You learned plenty of priceless principles on the previous pages. It's a lot to unpack and apply to your daily life, but it's my pleasure to fully endorse these effects, principles, and laws of the universe. I challenge you to implement this new paradigm shift, which is just to say that you can now ask better questions, do something more profound, and be someone more significant in this life of yours.

Thanks to this book, you are no longer asking yourself how to get more cash; you are asking yourself how to get more access and leverage. Thanks to these chapters, you can now attract more wealth and power to do good in the world. In many ways this is a little book designed to help you think big.

As someone who had the privilege to help write some of the words and design the visual aids on the previous pages, I developed quite a belief in not only Doria Cordova but also her mentors and associates. This is work that can't be stopped, and the world has been prepared for it. Place by place and country by country, this is the work spreading across every land, helping each one of us become self-reliant and self-sufficient.

Although I can't say that I know Doria best—not with so many that have shared her work for decades—I can say that over the last couple of years that I've spent with her researching her insights and the insights of the thought leaders who surround her, there is something truly special about her belief systems and her global work. It's been an honor to be a part of this publication. On behalf of everyone around the world, thank you!

David T. Fagan

www.DavidTFagan.com

David T. Fagan is the former CEO of Guerrilla Marketing, which sold over twenty-three million books in sixty-two languages all over the world, as well as the former owner of LCo Communications, a Beverly Hills PR firm that has represented fifty-eight Academy Award winners, thirty-four Grammy winners, and forty-three *New York Times* best sellers.

He has been featured on *Fox & Friends*, the *Today Show*, the *Washington Post, Forbes, Investor's Business Daily, Your World with Neil Cavuto*, Fox's *The Five*, and *What's Happening Now*, to name a few. He has won major awards for publishing, publicity, and even the Entrepreneur Educator of the Year Award from Inc 500 Infusionsoft.

David is the best-selling author of several books, including *Word Genius: What to Say and How to Say It; Guerrilla Parenting: How to Raise an Entrepreneur; Cracking the Icon Code: How to Become an Icon in Your Industry Through Your Advice, Image, and Expertise*; and *Becoming Significant: How to Invoke Sacred Words That Unlock Real Power.*

He's an international speaker in places as far away as Dubai, Bangladesh, Kenya, and Australia. He has shared the stage with everyone from former Secretary of Defense Dr. Bob Gates to Mark Victor Hansen.

David is the father of eight children (four girls and four boys) and has three grandchildren. He's married to Isabel Donadio-Fagan, and they live in the Phoenix, Arizona, area.

Thank you for reading this book!

Since 1979, Excellerated Business School® for Entrepreneurs, Money & You®, and other Excellerated programs have had 200,000-plus graduates from more than 85 countries, with a focus on the Americas and the Asia Pacific region.

The programs have been held in English in the United States, Canada, Australia, New Zealand, Hong Kong, Singapore, Malaysia, and India (with Tamil translation).

The programs have also been held in Chinese, both in Mandarin and Cantonese, in Taiwan, China, Singapore, Malaysia, Indonesia, Philippines, Thailand, and Canada through the Doers Group organizations which have put the Excellerated programs on the Chinese map.

They have recently been presented in Japan and Vietnam (both with translation). The program has also been presented in Spanish (with translation) and is now being launched in additional Spanish markets, as well as the Bahasa-speaking world.

Visit www.MoneyAndYou.com to learn more and view the global schedule.

Please contact us at Info@MoneyandYou.com if you have any questions or inquiries, or need support.

+1-619-224-8880 (Call, Text, SMS, WhatsApp).

We wish you tremendous success, health, prosperity, peace,

and joy in your business and personal endeavors, as you continue to have a positive impact on the world through your products, services, and programs that benefit everyone.

About the Author

Excellerated Business School® for Entrepreneurs, Money & You®, and other *Excellerated* programs are owned by Dame Doria (DC) Cordova, Ph.D. (Hon.).

Many of today's wealth and business leaders around the world have attended the *Money & You* program, which has transformed the way they teach, their choices in how to have a greater positive impact in the world, and how to integrate the win/win/win principles taught in the programs into their organizations.

Dame Cordova's work has touched the lives of tens of millions around the world, as a result of these graduates, including her nine-year business partnership (1985-1994) with Robert T. Kiyosaki of *Rich Dad Poor Dad* fame and his then-wife, Kim Kiyosaki. The essence of her work is to create learning environments in which established, successful, and emerging entrepreneurs, professionals, and educators are encouraged to focus not only on the bottom line and profits, but also on creating products, services, and programs that add value to humanity.

In the late 1970s, she was the only Latina among a group of pioneers led by Marshall Thurber and Bobbi DePorter who began the development of the entrepreneurial, experiential, transformational training industry. On July 8, 1985, she inherited the work, which has grown to what it is today thanks to countless partners, associates, teams, and the support of many graduates and friends.

Dame Cordova and the Kiyosakis established this training industry in the Asia Pacific region in 1985, first in Australia, then in New Zealand, and finally in Singapore. From late 1994, she expanded her training platform throughout the Asia Pacific and other markets in partnership with extraordinary promotional partners.

Many of today's transformational leaders have participated in *Excellerated* programs and have gone on to replicate and expand the *Excellerated* experiential educational methods. This has aided the ongoing education of financial literacy for the general public around the world. The work of her many graduates has helped to spread the essence of this mission to tens of millions of people globally. Her *Money & You* program's notable graduates read like a Who's Who of today's wealth and financial literacy experts.

Because the *Excellerated Business Schools, Money & You,* and other *Excellerated* programs have activated, inspired, and motivated so many successful, socially responsible entrepreneurs to act on behalf of humanity, her work makes a significant contribution to planetary evolutionary transformation.

She is the only Latina leader in an industry that has grown into a global organization with a licensing model that has given her the independence to expand her business ventures into renewables and continue her humanitarian efforts for over four decades. She has achieved this level of success by utilizing the numerous tools, principles, and systems taught in the *Excellerated* programs and in her publications.

Her stated purpose is to "uplift humanity's consciousness through socially responsible business." Leading by example, Doria is a philanthropist and humanitarian and is known as an *Ambassador of New Education*, with a tireless pursuit to transform educational systems around the world and eradicate poverty and hunger.

She serves as a mentor and champion for several of non-profits, foundations, and humanitarian organizations. She is now leading this work through the *Doria Cordova Foundation*. As of this writing, one of her projects is to encourage and inspire 100 billionaires to invest $1 billion each to feed the hungry and, eventually, eradicate global hunger.

Doria is a *Mentor of Nurturing* because of her work with high-level entrepreneurs and business leaders. She is a connector with a special talent for bringing together diverse, successful, global social entrepreneurs.

Doria's work has expanded to include renewable energy. She's a global business developer for Huang Ming, one of the world's leading renewables pioneers who built the only Solar Valley in the world in Dezhou, China. Ming, dubbed a "billionaire with heart," is a recipient of the *Right Livelihood Award* (the alternative to the Nobel Prize) and was instrumental in the passage of the first Green Law in China.

Doria is a visiting professor at *International Micro-emission University*, the world's first university dedicated to educating young students, professionals, entrepreneurs, and anyone else interested in studying and learning about the renewable energy industry.

Doria's tireless effort to persuade nations to adopt workable energy and its fair and equitable distribution so that all people can live in healthy environments, prosperity and Earth's wellness is reflected in her promotion of green technologies.

She is one of the contributors to the *Think & Grow Rich for Women* book. She is the author of *Money-Making Systems*, a comprehensive manual that any organization can use and create income-generating systems.

She has contributed to and written forewords for numerous books. Doria has appeared in a slew of motivational films, television shows, and online programs. She has been interviewed in all forms of media all over the world, hosted the *Money & You* radio show, and is a sought-after speaker at summits and conferences all over the world.

She is the author of the *Money & You book* series, which offers tools, techniques, and principles for achieving financial and personal success.

Doria began supporting her global network with various programs following the global paradigm shift caused by the COVID-19 pandemic, and those events evolved into the *Fridays with Doria & Friends* global platform, which now has a plethora of excellent teachings from experts who freely share their mastery, strategies, and knowledge with all who desire to further their entrepreneurial journey.

Doria is working on her dream, the *Excellerated Online University*, a platform that will include the many mentors and masters she encounters daily in her entrepreneurial and humanitarian endeavors.

Doria's next project is a global women's platform called *Women, Cash, and Divine Matters.* A global, multicultural online platform for women to connect and support one another will be a critical component of this work. It will also provide mentorship, coaching, inspiration, and hands-on business education.

Doria's various platforms spread the word about the importance of global entrepreneurship. The time has come for businesses of all sizes to recognize the value of global connectivity in expanding their markets, broadening their influence, and taking collective responsibility for the well-being of all people on Earth.

She is active on many social media platforms and thoroughly enjoys keeping up with the latest technological marvels that allow for the dissemination of information that promotes a world that works for 100% of humanity and works to shift the world from a scarcity paradigm to a sufficiency paradigm, thereby creating resources for all who lack them.

She is a founding member of the *Transformational Leadership Council* and the *Southern California Association of Transformational Leaders*; a board member of the *Evolutionary Business Council*; an international business development adviser for the *California Women's Conference*, and *Touchpointe*, a platform designed to bridge medical and holistic/alternative medicine; and an advisor/mentor to several other for-profit and non-profit organizations that benefit humanity.

Doria was knighted as Dame of Honor by the *Sovereign Order of the Orthodox Knights Hospitaller of Saint John of Jerusalem* in 2010 on her birthday, November 14, for her lifelong service to humanity. She was promoted to Dame Commander of Grace in January 2013 and to Chancellor of the California Priory of the Order in 2018 for her contributions to the order's growth.

Doria received an Honorary Doctorate in Wealth Wellness with a specialization in Transformational Leadership from the *Indian Virtual University for Peace and Education*, which is registered with the *United Nations* and accredited by the *Indian Council for Professional Education Mission*, on December 18, 2016.

Doria never had her own children, but she is a godmother to many around the world, supports several orphanages, and has four "bonus grandchildren" as of this writing. Children hold a special place in her heart, and her dream is for no child anywhere in the world to go to bed hungry. She lives in San Diego, California, and Maui, Hawaii, with her beloved, Christian Mentzel, when she is not traveling.

Her true home is Spaceship Earth.

To Find Out More About the Author

Website

https://MeetDoria.com

Social Networking Sites

https://www.linkedin.com/in/dccordova/

https://www.facebook.com/DCCordova

https://www.facebook.com/DCCordovaFriends

https://www.instagram.com/damedccordova/

https://twitter.com/dccordova

https://twitter.com/moneyandyou

https://www.facebook.com/moneyandyou

https://www.youtube.com/@DameDCCordova

https://www.youtube.com/@MoneyAndYouEducation

Clubhouse: @DoriaCordova - Follow *Money & You Club*

Resources

Free Entrepreneurial Training

Excellerated Business Success Model E-book

A tried-and-true formula for establishing successful and profitable businesses. Learn financial success principles, tools, and systems. Live a prosperous and productive life that contributes to the betterment of humanity.

Download at: https://moneyandyou.com

Fridays with Doria & Friends, Global Platform

Meet our global network and increase your power, influence, impact, and wealth. Replays of business and entrepreneurial masters and experts are available. Ho'oponopono prayers are also offered to the global network.

https://fridayswithdoria.com

Magical Recovery Exercises

Successful transformational financial masters, experts, and best-selling authors have completed this process. Do these simple exercises to help you clear multigenerational financial decisions activated during the global paradigm shift or simply in the process of life:

https://fridayswithdoria.com/magicalexercises/

Excellerated Live Programs

Money & You Program – Live Signature Program for Three and a half days

Consists of 65% experiential exercises that teach you how to peel back the layers of success, wealth, and business-building breakthroughs to put yourself on a path to a better life:

https://www.moneyandyou.com

Global Excellerated Business School for Entrepreneurs (BSE)

This is the program that, in 1978, gave birth to the entrepreneurial, experiential, transformational industry. Today's curriculum focuses on some of the world's hottest trends and fastest-growing industries, including new technologies, renewables, and impact:

https://www.globalexcelleratedbusinessschool.com

Doria Cordova Foundation

For decades, Dame Doria Cordova, her partners, and affiliated organizations have been doing philanthropic work. This foundation will be the steward of this work as she enters the legacy stage of her life and continues to fulfill her life's purpose:

https://doriacordovafoundation.org

Online Education

Access to Cash Online Entrepreneurial Course

Six-and-a-half-hours of distinctions, strategies, and tools from Doria Cordova's forty-plus years of experience to support you to create a profitable business or non-profit organization:

https://accesstocashcourse.com

Money-Making Systems Manual

"Excellerate" your entrepreneurial skills by organizing your office, desk, computer, apps used in your organization. The nuts and bolts of forming teams and increasing your productivity:

https://www.moneyandyou.com/money-making-systems/

Leverage: Key to Access to Cash

Simple and straightforward online course for learning distinctions for leveraging your time, money, resources, networks, and energy!

https://www.leverageto.cash

Evolve Experience: Two-Day Online Live Event

This global live online event will connect you with extraordinary entrepreneurs and help you expand your global markets. The exercises in the program are both interactive and transformational:

http://MoneyandYou.com/EvolveXP

Reading List & Gifts Available

https://www.accesstocashbook.com/reading/

Many books have positively influenced, impacted, and inspired Dame Doria Cordova (and many others) to lead, run, and expand her businesses and personal life.

Money & You graduates and friends are constantly becoming best-selling authors; a comprehensive list can be found at www.AccessToCashBook.com where you can also download gifts.

Congratulations, *Money & You* graduates, on your best-selling books. Please contact us at info@moneyandyou.com if you wish to be added to our Reading List!

Thank you… Good luck in applying the principles taught in this publication… and May The Force Be With You!

Made in the USA
Monee, IL
12 November 2026

88070da8-2b58-4a51-a1e3-4f3286f0ad91R01